Birthday

Julie Murray

Abdo
HOLIDAYS
Kids

abdopublishing.com

Published by Abdo Kids, a division of ABDO, PO Box 398166, Minneapolis, Minnesota 55439.
Copyright © 2018 by Abdo Consulting Group, Inc. International copyrights reserved in all countries.
No part of this book may be reproduced in any form without written permission from the publisher.

Printed in the United States of America, North Mankato, Minnesota.

102017

012018

THIS BOOK CONTAINS
RECYCLED MATERIALS

Photo Credits: Alamy, Getty Images, iStock, Shutterstock

Production Contributors: Teddy Borth, Jennie Forsberg, Grace Hansen

Design Contributors: Christina Doffing, Candice Keimig, Dorothy Toth

Publisher's Cataloging in Publication Data

Names: Murray, Julie, author.
Title: Birthday / by Julie Murray.
Description: Minneapolis, Minnesota : Abdo Kids, 2018. | Series: Holidays |
           Includes glossary, index and online resource (page 24).
Identifiers: LCCN 2017942858 | ISBN 9781532103902 (lib.bdg.) | ISBN 9781532105029 (ebook) |
           ISBN 9781532105586 (Read-to-me ebook)
Subjects: LCSH: Holidays--Juvenile literature. | Birthday--Juvenile literature. |
           Celebrations--Juvenile literature.
Classification: DDC 394.2--dc23
LC record available at https://lccn.loc.gov/2017942858

Table of Contents

Birthday

Your birthday is **special**. It is
the day you were born.

It is a day to celebrate!

Kate blows up balloons.

Lynne's mom makes a cake.

She **decorates** it.

8

Emma hits the piñata.

Candy falls out.

The kids sing a song. It is "Happy Birthday to You."

Adam blows out his candle.

Time to eat cake.

It is fun to open gifts.

Everyone is excited!

16

Sara opens the mail. It is a birthday card!

Ana loves her birthday!

21

Signs of a Birthday

balloons

cake

cards

gifts

Glossary

celebrate
to make special or honor with gifts, parties, or activities.

decorate
to make more beautiful by adding decorations or designs.

special
out of the ordinary.

Index

Abdo Kids
ONLINE
FREE! ONLINE MULTIMEDIA RESOURCES

Visit **abdokids.com** and use this code to access crafts, games, videos, and more!

Abdo Kids Code:
HBK3902

24